MY BROTHER ZANE

BY
LORETTA WOODS

ILLUSTRATIONS BY
EMINENCE SYSTEM

MY BROTHER ZANE

Illustrations by Eminence System

1405 SW 6th Avenue • Ocala, Florida 34471 • Phone 352-622-1825 • Fax 352-622-1875
Website: www.atlantic-pub.com • Email: sales@atlantic-pub.com
SAN Number: 268-1250

Library of Congress Control Number: 2020922608

Printed in the United States

PROJECT MANAGER: Crystal Edwards
INTERIOR LAYOUT AND JACKET DESIGN: Nicole Sturk

This book is dedicated to
ZEILA.

Don't let anyone keep you from making a difference
and standing up for what's right.

Hi! My name is JAZMIN. I love roller skating. It took me a long time to learn but I finally got it. Apart from roller skating, I love reading, giving my best friend Maria math problems to solve, and playing soccer with my little brother, Zane.

This is my brother, ZANE. He is younger than me. Zane is a neat kid. He loves sports and science experiments. One time he created a rocket with a plastic bottle and baking soda. Zane says he wants to be a *scienceballenier*. My parents are still trying to figure out what that means. I think he wants to create ways to use balls to do really cool stuff.

My best friend's name is **MARIA**. She lives in our neighborhood. She likes science too, and she has a brother too. She says her brother is a real smarty-pants. "He is cool," Zane says.

WE PLAY TOGETHER outside often. We make up games, and sometimes talk about going to space together. When we play soccer, we play in teams. Sometimes it's Zane and Maria playing against me. Sometimes it's Maria and me playing against Zane.

Sometimes we get into **TROUBLE**. It's always an accident.
We don't like getting into trouble.

MOM always seems to get mad at Zane more than she gets mad at me. Mom seems to worry more about Zane than she does about me. Maria says her mom acts like that about her brother, too.

"It **WASN'T ONLY YOUR FAULT**, Zane. Sorry, baby brother."

One day, **DADDY** told me that they treat Zane differently for a couple of reasons. Daddy said, "Zane is a brown boy, and the world will be more mad at him if he makes mistakes. Sorry, baby girl, that's just the way it is right now."

I didn't think that was fair. **I DIDN'T UNDERSTAND.**
I just listened as questions floated through my head.

"Try not to worry, JAZMIN.
Things will be okay," Daddy assured me.

DAD said people are fighting to make this better. People
are speaking up when they see something wrong. People are
standing up for what is right. People are using the law to look
at how brown boys are being treated.

I can do these things too. **I WILL PROTECT HIM.** I will love Zane, and make sure others know he is lovable. I will not let the world get mad at him because he is a brown boy. Mom and Dad say they are proud of me. They are proud of me for trying to make a change.

Why was Jazmin worried about Zane?

Why do you think Zane's mom was mad at him, even though it wasn't only his fault the flower pot was knocked down?

Why was Zane sad?

Do you think females and males are treated differently?

Have you noticed or heard that black and white people are treated differently?

What can you do to make a change?

How can you help make sure people are treated fairly?

www.ingramcontent.com/pod-product-compliance
Lightning Source LLC
Chambersburg PA
CBHW061416090426

42742CB00026B/3483